The Many-Sided Cross

Sermons and Orders
of Service for Lent

By Cynthia E. Cowen

C.S.S. Publishing Company, Inc.
Lima, Ohio

THE MANY-SIDED CROSS

Copyright © 1991 by
The C.S.S. Publishing Company, Inc.
Lima, Ohio

All rights reserved. No part of this publication may be reproduced, stored in a retrieval system, or transmitted in any form or by any means, electronic, mechanical, photocopying, recording, or otherwise, without the prior permission of the publisher. Inquiries should be addressed to: The C.S.S. Publishing Company, Inc., 628 South Main Street, Lima, Ohio 45804.

Library of Congress Cataloging-in-Publication Data

Cowen, Cynthia E., 1947-
  The many-sided cross: sermons and orders of worship for Lent / by Cynthia E. Cowen.
    p.   cm.
  ISBN 1-55673-285-6
  1. Lenten sermons. 2. Holy-Week sermons. 3. Easter—Sermons.
4. Sermons, American 5. Worship programs. 6. Easter service.
I. Title.
BV4277.C59   1991
264—dc20   90-46981
                                                             CIP

9118 / ISBN 1-55673-285-6   PRINTED IN U.S.A.

These resources came about through prayer and are dedicated to Lloyd and Grace Scholl, two prayer warriors in their eighties, who love the church and its pastors. They gave my then seminary student husband a book, *The Many Sided Cross, A Personal Retreat* by William R. Seaman, now deceased, which was an excellent devotional guide during Lent for us. Prayer brought my spouse through an illness, but the illness enabled me to plug into God's creative energy and produce the material. "And we know that in all things God works for the good of those who love him, who have been called according to his purpose."

Romans 8:28

Table of Contents

Ash Wednesday
　Order of Service 7
　The Cross of Repentance 11

Palm Sunday
　Order of Service 17
　The Cross of Salvation 20

Maundy Thursday
　Order of Service 25
　The Cross of Destiny 29

Good Friday
　Order of Service 33
　The Cross of Commitment 37

Easter Vigil
　Order of Service 43
　Crossroads 48

Easter Sunrise
　Order of Service 53
　What's On Your Easter Menu? 57

THE MANY-SIDED CROSS
ASH WEDNESDAY SERVICE

Prelude
Welcome and Announcements

LITANY OF THE CROSS

*(P) Brothers and sisters: As we begin our Lenten journey to the cross, we recognize that sin separates us from the love of God. We cannot enjoy the life meant for us by God until we are reconciled to him. The sacrifice for that reconciliation has been provided for us in the death of Christ. All who turn to the cross and embrace that sacrifice will have eternal life with him.

(C) "**FOR GOD SO LOVED THE WORLD THAT HE GAVE HIS ONLY BEGOTTEN SON THAT WHOEVER BELIEVES IN HIM MIGHT NOT PERISH BUT HAVE EVERLASTING LIFE.**"

(P) Most holy and merciful Father:

(C) **WE COME TO THE FOOT OF THE CROSS TONIGHT AND CONFESS TO YOU, TO OUR BROTHERS AND SISTERS IN FAITH, AND TO THE ENTIRE COMMUNITY IN HEAVEN AND EARTH THAT WE HAVE NOT BEEN FAITHFUL IN ALL OUR WAYS. WE HAVE SINNED AGAINST YOU, O LORD, IN THOUGHT, WORD, AND DEED IN THOSE THINGS WE HAVE DONE AND LEFT UNDONE.**

(P) Lord, as we draw closer to the cross of Christ, we realize that we have not loved you with our whole heart, mind, and strength. As we look upon your body on that cross, we realize that we have not loved our neighbors as ourselves. You laid down your life for us as a sacrifice for the forgiveness of our sins. As we turn to the cross and receive that forgiveness, we realize that we have not forgiven others as we have been forgiven.

(C) **LORD, HAVE MERCY ON US.**
(Silence for reflection and self-examination)

SERVICE OF THE WORD

*Opening Hymn
First Reading: Joel 2:12-19
Psalm 51:1-13 (Sung or read responsively)
Second Reading: Matthew 6:1-6
Lenten Meditation: "The Cross of Repentance"
Solo or Anthem
Offering
Offertory

WE STEP TOWARD THE CROSS

*(P) Our first step toward the cross is through repentance.
(C) **OUR HEART CRIES OUT TO YOU, LORD.**
(P) God's first step toward us is with forgiveness.
(C) **OUR HEART CRIES OUT TO YOU, LORD.**
(P) God comes to us in love as we hear the words of our Lord from the cross, "Father, forgive them, for they know not what they do."
(C) **OUR HEART CRIES OUT TO YOU, LORD.**
(P) In Christ's death upon the cross we are forgiven.
(C) **OUR SALVATION COMES FROM THE CROSS OF CHRIST.**

THE MANY-SIDED CROSS

*(P) The cross is salvation!
(C) **WE ARE REDEEMED BY CHRIST'S PRECIOUS BLOOD.**
(P) The cross is repentance!
(C) **GRANT US GRACE TO TURN FROM SIN.**
(P) The cross is forgiveness.
(C) **RESTORE US TO RELATIONSHIP WITH YOU, LORD.**

(P) The cross is love!
(C) **FILL US WITH YOUR LOVE.**
(P) The cross is freedom!
(C) **WE ARE FREED FROM THE BONDAGE OF SIN AND DEATH.**
(P) The cross is slavery!
(C) **WE ARE SLAVES TO GOD, CRUCIFIED WITH CHRIST.**
(P) The cross is mystery!
(C) **THOUGH WE SIN AGAINST YOU, LORD, GRANT US MERCY.**
(P) The cross is power!
(C) **FOR THE PREACHING OF THE CROSS IS, TO THEM WHO ARE PERISHING, FOOLISHNESS; BUT TO US WHO ARE SAVED, IT IS THE POWER OF GOD!**
(P) The cross is Life!
(C) **FOR TO ME, TO LIVE IS CHRIST AND TO DIE IS GAIN.**

WE SEE BEYOND THE CROSS

*(P) Having embraced the many sides of the cross, we come before you, Lord, in intercession for the needs of ourselves, our families, our church, our world.
(C) **HEAR THE PRAYERS OF OUR HEARTS, LORD.**

*Prayers of the Church

WE STEP TOWARD THE CROSS
THROUGH COMMUNION

*(P) The night in which Christ was betrayed, he took bread, gave thanks, broke it, and giving it to his disciples, said: Take and eat. This is my body given for you. Do this in remembrance of me. After the meal, he took the cup, gave thanks, and gave it to all to drink, saying: This cup is for the new covenant in my blood, shed for you and for all people for the forgiveness of sin. Do this in remembrance of me.

*Lord's Prayer
Distribution of Communion
*(P) Accomplish your perfect will in our lives, Lord, as we journey forth from here tonight.
(C) **MAY YOUR CROSS BE EVER BEFORE US THIS WEEK UNTIL WE MEET AGAIN TO SURVEY THE WONDER OF THAT PRECIOUS GIFT.**
*Benediction
*Closing Hymn

***Congregation Stands**

THE CROSS OF REPENTÁNCE

Ash Wednesday

Lessons: Psalm 51:1-13; Joel 2:12-19; Matthew 6:1-6

Mardi Gras! Festivals of light! Great crowds gathering to have fun. Costumes, dancing, the good times a'rolling! That's what occurs at this time of year in New Orleans, Rio de Janeiro, all over the world as people celebrate and load up on all those fats that Shrove Tuesday dishes out. Out East they celebrate Fascht Naucht (Fat Night) by cooking homemade donuts in bubbling fat, heaping heavy syrup on pancakes, and gorging themselves on high caloric goodies. This tradition comes from the Old World, where the night before Lent the family would use up all the fats in the pantry in preparation for a time of fasting. The focus in these situations is on enjoyment, celebration, filling your cup to the brim before "The Day." Well, today is "The Day." In the church we celebrate today as Ash Wednesday. The frivolity and merriment have died down. The feasts have left many with feelings of regret. The focus has abruptly changed. We now enter the season of Lent.

In order for us to switch our focus, it would be helpful to zero in on a physical object which would enable us to grasp hold of a focal point. For us in this Lenten series, it will be the cross. Crosses come in all shapes and sizes. Churches display a variety. Most are not one-sided. Some are large, wooden, displaying many angles where carpenters have arranged the pieces of wood to appeal to the eye. Some are a combination of metal and wood with bursts of ornamentation attached for decoration. Many today wear crosses which can be ornate, studded with jewels, simple gold or silver, crucifixes, wood, or crosses with doves or flames, or crosses of nails. The list can go on and on. The variety of the crosses reflects the differences in the ones who wear them, for they have usually been selected to make statements about piety. But have you ever given thought to the different aspects of the cross of Jesus Christ and its application to you?

Lent is a time to journey to the cross. The cross of Christ may be approached from many angles. In college, the cross is presented as history. In our seminaries, the cross is presented as theology. For missionaries, the cross is the gospel. For most, the cross is forgiveness. Some see the cross as prayer in time of necessity. The cross can be discipline. For priests, nuns, pastors, and all believers committed to the Lord Jesus, the cross is a way of life. The cross is comfort. The cross is sorrow. The cross is hope. The cross is mystery. The cross is death.

Thomas a Kempis, a great theologian, gives us a good summary of the cross. "In the cross is salvation, in the cross is life, in the cross is protection against our enemies, in the cross is strength of mind, in the cross is joy of spirit, in the cross is the height of virtue, in the cross is the perfection of holiness. There is no salvation of the soul, nor hope of everlasting life, but in the cross . . . Take up therefore thy cross and follow Jesus, and thou shalt go into life everlasting."

The cross for the Christian is the symbol of the sacrifice of Christ. It represents the tool which killed the Lamb of God. We cannot obtain salvation or hope of eternal life without recognizing the work of Christ upon that cross. The series we are about to embark on will deal with the many-sided cross. Tonight's journey begins with Ash Wednesday, traditionally a time for confession and absolution as we turn from our sins and acknowledge our need for a savior. The side of the cross we will examine first will be the cross of repentance, for there can be no journey to Easter morning without passing through Good Friday and lingering at the foot of the cross in repentance.

From our first reading we hear the words of the Lord, "Return to me with all your heart, with fasting, with weeping and with mourning; and rend your hearts and not your garments." The prophet calls upon God's people to repent, to turn the whole self to God, and perhaps, the calamity which is going to befall them might be averted. The calamity for us is a life separated from God. A life that sees no hope. A life that does not lead to salvation, but to judgment and damnation. That is the end result of an unrepentant life. The seeds we sow in this life will bear the fruits we will have to eat in the next. When we sow bitterness, hatred, deceitfulness, or injustice, why should we expect to be filled with any different fruits in the next life? When we live our lives separated from God, why should we expect to live eternally united with him following our death? Any life — this one or the next — spent separated from our Lord and Savior — is a life of darkness, of hopelessness — a living hell.

Is that, therefore, the basis of the prophet's call to repentance? Is it the action of the people that will cause God to change his mind? This prophet states that it is the reverse. Repentance is based on God's prior action to and for his people. Our Father is merciful and gracious. David pleas from our psalm tonight, confirming that: "Have mercy on me, O God, according to your unfailing love; according to your great compassion, blot out my transgressions." He recognizes the qualities of mercy and compassion that God gives to his children. Uppermost in the mind of God is the well-being of his people. God loved his people so much that he continued to call them to himself in love through his prophets. He calls to us today through Jesus. God's action rooted in the death and resurrection of Jesus Christ establishes a relationship of trust and obedience between our Creator and his creations. Living in this personal relationship with him, we are called to the cross of repentance not just tonight, but throughout our lives. Salvation is based upon that love for us, because God first loved us through Jesus, his death and resurrection. God judges us in the face of the cross of repentance. Choosing to live an unrepentant life makes an enemy of the cross in our denial of God's purpose of salvation. But because God loves us, he will not force us or beat us or scare us into the decision of embracing the cross of Christ. Accepting the gift of salvation in Christ by believing in Jesus and repenting of our sinfulness is a matter of our own free election.

To believe, we know, is to put our whole love and trust in Jesus the Christ. But what is this thing that we call "repentance?" Why do we first need to look at the cross from this angle?

"I'm sorry," we have often heard others as well as ourselves say. As children, we learn quickly that a well placed "I'm sorry" will avert the hand of punishment. All too soon that phrase loses its significance and simply becomes part of our everyday vocabulary. The phrase becomes trite when no time is spent in reflection upon it. Whether as children or adults, we do not like to face our mistakes or sins. There are scores of books and articles written to encourage us as individuals to feel good about ourselves. They may even suggest that serious reflection on our mistakes is a downer that we don't need in life. Isn't saying "I'm sorry" good enough?

No! It is not! To repent means to feel remorse or self-reproach for what we have done or failed to do. It also means that we want to change our lives so as not to repeat the mistakes of the past.

Repentance is a spiritual, physical, and emotional experience that corrects our relationship with God. Repentance removes the barriers that we, ourselves, have put up between ourselves and God. Repentance is not an option that we may take or leave. It is a must, the first step toward the cross. If we wish to be close to our Lord and Savior, we must take that initial step toward Calvary.

Jesus describes for us how to take this step toward repentance in our gospel. There are three aspects involved: denial of self (almsgiving), prayer, and fasting. Certainly an essential part of repentance is the denial of self. The gospel speaks of the posture, the manner, to be taken when giving. We know that on our own, we are totally unworthy of salvation. There is absolutely nothing we can do to win God's forgiveness. As repentant Christians, our response to the gift of salvation is giving. We give, we share, we serve because we were first served and given to. One part of the uneasiness of repentance is our attitude about that giving. Tonight's gospel concludes with the reminder "for where your treasure is, there your heart will be also." Repentance requires that we seek God's will and ways, and not the approval or admiration of the crowd. God's will revealed in Jesus Christ must be where our treasure lies.

Repentance also involves prayer. We need to converse daily with God. Prayer is that form of conversation. One of its many parts needs to be the asking of forgiveness. The gospel reminds us that prayer is not done to impress the public, but to reconcile our broken relationship with God. We need to evaluate our prayers. If they have become an easy "I'm sorry," and we no longer feel the sting of our sin, then we need to do some honest, hard work. Through thoughtful examination of the spiritual condition of our souls in prayer, we need to seek God's will for us as we earnestly confess and receive forgiveness. We need to linger at the foot of the cross and view it from the proper angle. We need to sit still long enough to get the right perspective on our attitude toward sin and Christ. We need to pause long enough to hear the words, "Father, forgive them." For in hearing those words, we will cry out, "Forgive me."

In the ancient church, fasting was also an important part of repentance and preparation during the Lenten season. It was seen as a spiritual discipline. Often it meant only one meal per day, spending the rest of the day in prayer. Fasting was also to be a vivid reminder of what Jesus endured for our salvation. In an era of instant gratification, such a pause could greatly improve our spiritual health.

Humans have always had the tendency to be lazy and to avoid responsibility. Modern society seems to put a great emphasis on having a good time, regardless of the moral issues involved. All of us are tempted to ignore God's will and serve our own. We are tempted to leap to Easter morning without stopping at the cross of Good Friday. Therefore, Ash Wednesday is the time to stop the running and the denial. Tonight we need to honestly begin the process of working on repentance. In this Lenten season, may we grasp the many angles of the cross of Christ. Let us repent and believe, for in that call we will obtain eternal life through the death and resurrection of Jesus Christ. Isn't that gift worth a whole lot more than a casual "I'm sorry?"

May the cross of repentance be engraved upon our hearts and minds tonight and linger throughout the week, until we gaze upon the cross again from a different angle. In his precious name. Amen.

THE MANY-SIDED CROSS
PALM SUNDAY CELEBRATION

Prelude

BLESSING OF THE PALMS

*(P) We stand before the Lord of Hosts, proclaiming God's faithfulness as he secured for us a plan of salvation. May the praises we raise today echo down through the centuries joining those who hailed him on his triumphal entry into Jerusalem. Bless these palms we now hold as they are waved in celebration, announcing the coming of the King of kings, Jesus the Christ.

(C) **WE BLESS YOU, O LORD!**

THE PALMS SPEAK OUT GOD'S PLAN
**(Litany based on the Gospel of
Matthew 20:17-19 and Matthew 21:1-11)**

*(P) Blessed is he who comes in the name of the Lord.

(C) **HOSANNA TO THE SON OF DAVID!**

(P) Now as Jesus was going up to Jerusalem, he took the 12 disciples aside and said to them, "we are going up to Jerusalem, and the Son of Man will be betrayed to the chief priests and the teachers of the law. They will condemn him to death and will turn him over to the gentiles to be mocked and flogged and crucified. On the third day he will be raised to life!"

(C) **LORD GOD, WE RECOGNIZE THE NEED TO RECONCILE US TO YOURSELF. PRAISE GOD FOR THE PLAN OF SALVATION!**

(P) As they approached Jerusalem and came to Bethphage on the Mount of Olives, Jesus sent two disciples, saying to them, "Go to the village ahead of you, and at once you will find a donkey tied there, with her colt by her. Untie them and bring them to me. If anyone says anything to you, tell him that the Master has need of them, and he will send them right away."

(C) **LORD GOD, AS YOU CAME TO US IN HUMILITY, WE RECOGNIZE THAT YOUR LOVE IS AVAILABLE TO ALL PEOPLE. PRAISE GOD FOR THE PLAN OF SALVATION!**
(P) This took place to fulfill what was spoken through the prophet: "Say to the Daughter of Zion, 'Behold, your king comes to you, gentle and riding on a donkey, on a colt, the foal of a donkey.' "
(C) **LORD GOD, WE RECOGNIZE YOUR FAITHFULNESS IN FULFILLING YOUR WORD. PRAISE GOD FOR THE PLAN OF SALVATION!**
(P) The disciples went and did as Jesus had instructed them. They brought the donkey and the colt, placed their cloaks on them, and Jesus sat on them. A very large crowd spread their cloaks on the road, while others cut branches from the trees and spread them on the road.
(C) **LORD GOD, WE RECOGNIZE OUR NEED TO PAY HOMAGE TO OUR KING. PRAISE GOD FOR THE PLAN OF SALVATION!**
(P) The crowds that went ahead of him and those that followed shouted:
(C) **HOSANNA TO THE SON OF DAVID! BLESSED IS HE WHO COMES IN THE NAME OF THE LORD! HOSANNA IN THE HIGHEST!**
(P) When Jesus entered Jerusalem, the whole city was stirred and asked, "Who is this?" The crowds answered:
(C) **THIS IS JESUS, THE PROPHET FROM NAZARETH IN GALILEE.**
(P) The palms speak today as we wave them on high,
(C) **LORD GOD, WE NEED JESUS OUR KING! PRAISE GOD FOR THE PLAN OF SALVATION!**

*Processional Hymn

*(P) Blessed is he who comes in the name of the Lord.
(C) **HOSANNA IN THE HIGHEST!**

*(P) Let us pray: Lord God, we come before your throne of grace, throwing ourselves upon your mercy. Receive the cries from our humble hearts as we turn to acknowledge the salvation secured for us in the death of your Son, Jesus, on the cross. In our need for forgiveness, we embrance the cross of salvation. Fill us now with your love and joy as we raise our praise to the Son on high.
(C) **HOSANNA IN THE HIGHEST! AMEN.**

GOD'S HOLY WORD IS PROCLAIMED

Responsive Reading of Psalm 31:1-5, 9-16
First Lesson: Zechariah 9:9-10
Special Music
Second Lesson: Philippians 2:5-11
Hymn of the Day
Meditation: "The Cross of Salvation"

AN OFFERING OF PRAISE AND THANKSGIVING

*The Apostles' Creed
The Offering
Announcements
*The Offertory Response
*The Prayers of the Church
 (P) We join our hearts in offering up to God the prayers of community . . . Lord in your mercy,
 (C) **HEAR OUR PRAYER.**
*Lord's Prayer
*Benediction
*Recessional Hymn
*Postlude

*Congregation Stands

THE CROSS OF SALVATION

Palm Sunday

Lessons: Psalm 31:1-5, 9-16; Zechariah 9:9-10;
  Philippians 2:5-11;
  Matthew 20:17-19, 21:1-11

Anyone who has ever taken time to construct a jigsaw puzzle knows what an intricate and time-consuming project it is. Selecting edge pieces, one begins to connect them, building a framework and adding interlocking parts which continue to create a bigger picture. Checking the picture on the cover of the box, the puzzle-solver looks for like colors which can be assembled together. A spotted giraffe's neck certainly would not fit on the grey body of an elephant. Time passes as the picture begins to take shape, and the reward to solving the puzzle is a completed scene and a sense of satisfaction for the effort put in.

God has been at work throughout history creating intricate patterns and connecting bits and pieces which reveal to us a fascinating puzzle: the mystery of salvation. He has invested a lot of time and personal effort in this project. The framework was his love for the world as he brought creation into being. The picture was perfect. Creation lived in harmony with the Creator, but then sin entered the scene. Like a soda being spilled on a jigsaw puzzle, the perfect-picture paradise in the Garden of Eden was blotched and discolored by sin and disobedience as the pieces became disconnected and scattered. So God left the framework of his love and reconstructed the scene, taking a great deal of time and effort at reconciling his creations to himself once more.

Throughout time, God has been providing pieces of the puzzle for us, his puzzle-solvers, to connect. Today we see a corner of that puzzle take shape as Christ enters Jerusalem.

We see a picture of Jesus, our humble king, the one God chose to send into the world as the central piece to this puzzle of salvation. But in order to get a clearer picture, we need to go back and examine some of the other pieces to which we connect this Palm Sunday piece.

The Old Testament is full of the parts to our puzzle. They came in a variety of shapes and colors and were called prophets. They declared God's promises to his chosen people, foretelling the Savior's birth — even placing into the puzzle that piece which would tell where the Savior would be born: "But you, Bethlehem Ephrathah, though you are small among the clans of Judah, out of you will come one who will be ruler over Israel," the prophet Micah declared. Isaiah puzzled many with his declaration, "The virgin will be with child and will give birth to a son and will call him Immanuel." The puzzle took shape in God's time and with many pieces working together to make the picture more complete.

The picture grew clearer as God fitted more pieces together. We see the next piece of the puzzle put into place. Christ, who was with God at Creation and who reigned with the Father on high, voluntarily emptied himself of his kingship, humbling himself, becoming obedient to God's plan of salvation as he entered the world. Salvation took human form in the babe of Bethlehem.

The angels announced Christ's birth: "Today in the town of David a Savior has been born to you. He is Christ the Lord." Salvation had come to the world! When Jesus was presented at the temple, Simeon announced God's messenger, the one the prophets had declared, had arrived: "Sovereign Lord, as you have promised, dismiss now your servant in peace. For my eyes have seen your salvation." Salvation had come to the lost and waiting!

An important part of the puzzle was the prophet, John the Baptist, who prepared the way for Christ. John announced God's kingdom was at hand: "Look, the Lamb of God, who takes away the sin of the world." The sacrifice in human form stood before John to be baptized. "Salvation is near! Repent and believe the good news!" Christ would begin announcing after his baptism by John.

Christ's ministry was another piece of the puzzle which demonstrated God's love for all people. He announced the kingdom had come through demonstrations of power and miracles. Christ announced to John's disciples that he was the one John proclaimed. "Go back and report to John what you have seen and heard: The blind receive sight, the lame walk, those who have leprosy are cured, the deaf hear, the dead are raised, and the good news is preached to the poor." He proclaimed salvation with the Word as he taught and showed God's love. Salvation had come to hurting, sin-stained people!

As these pieces of the puzzle came together, it was time to add another, Palm Sunday. With green branches strewn before our king, Jesus rode in humility upon a donkey, announcing salvation was within the reach of all. Salvation had come for all people. Catch the vision of this piece of the puzzle of our salvation: Christ rode into Holy Week connected to God and us through love. The one who had entered Bethlehem in the womb of Mary, who was born in a humble stable, now entered Jerusalem, riding on a donkey. Our Savior came in a love that reaches out to you. The puzzle is almost complete.

The next pieces are fitted together quickly as the shouts of hosanna faded as Jesus confronted the sins of the people he came to save. Looking for the fruit of repentance, he found people chose to embrace the darkness of the world. The light of their salvation burned too intently for them to embrace. But God continued to put the pieces together as Christ shared his last supper with his disciples in the form of bread and the wine, his body and blood which would soon secure salvation for the world. The commandment to love connected the disciples and us as pieces into the puzzle. We, as Christ's church, become connected to him through faith and to each other as we reach out to others with that good news. The church becomes the light shining in the darkness of a hurting and sin-filled world. We become the messengers, like the prophets, like the angels, like John, like Simeon, like the disciples, like

Christ himself, announcing salvation through our love and lives lived out in humility to the king.

Good Friday planted firmly into the middle of the puzzle the most painful but necessary piece of salvation: the cross — God's cross of salvation.

God has presented the perfect picture of salvation in Jesus and his death for us upon that cross. Our Scripture passages today frame that cross. On the way to the cross that Palm Sunday, Jesus declared he had come for all people by showing himself a God of humility, riding into Jerusalem on a borrowed beast of burden. At the time of the last supper, Jesus declared his love would be remembered through the bread and wine shared in communion with him as Lord. The garden, another piece of the puzzle, was where Christ asked God's will, not his own, be done as he surrendered to the cross. Then the darkest pieces of our puzzle take form: "the betrayal," "the arrest," "the trial," "the scourging," "the crucifixion." Next Sunday the piece of light will be added: "the resurrection."

As we stand on this side of the cross and look back, we marvel at the love of our God who is so patient with us, his wayward children. He invests so much time and effort into demonstrating that love for us. The puzzle continues to come together and build as each of us hears the announcement of salvation and responds to the cross, becoming a part of the final piece, "the church."

When Christ returns, we will stand before him, the King who loves us and died for us, and sing his praises for all eternity. Until then, we stand before him this Palm Sunday and strew our palms of thanksgiving with our lips and in our hearts and through our lives as we personally announce that the King has come into our midst and salvation is secured. Jesus rides into our hearts and into our lives as our Lord, not just this day, but every day of our existence here on earth.

Behold, our King comes humbly announcing salvation for all people. He rides on a donkey, on a colt, the foal of a donkey. Ride on, Jesus. Ride on in majesty!

May this Palm Sunday sharpen our vision of the mystery of the puzzle of salvation as we ride on into the rest of Holy Week. In his holy name, Amen.

THE MÁNY-SIDED CROSS
MÁUNDY THURSDÁY CELEBRÁTION

Prelude
Silent Reflection

WE VIEW THE CROSS OF CHRIST

*(P) We look upon the Cross of Calvary;
(C) **WE SEE THE CROSS, OUR SALVATION!**
(P) We look from sin to life in Christ;
(C) **WE SEE THE CROSS IN REPENTANCE!**
(P) We look to be restored to God;
(C) **WE SEE THE CROSS AS FORGIVENESS!**
(P) We look upon the cross in shame;
(C) **WE SEE THE CROSS OF LOVE!**
(P) We look beyond the cross to eternal life;
(C) **WE SEE THE CROSS OF HOPE!**
(P) We look to Christ to set us free;
(C) **WE SEE THE CROSS OF FREEDOM!**
(P) We look for answers everywhere;
(C) **WE SEE A CROSS OF MYSTERY!**
(P) We know that we must die someday;
(C) **WE SEE THE CROSS OF LIFE!**

*Invocation
(P) Almighty God, you passed over Egypt that fateful night, saving those who had applied blood to their doorposts and beans from the Angel of Death. Apply the blood of Christ now to our lives in this celebration service. We call upon Jesus, the perfect Lamb, to be present at our feast. We remember with shame the need for his death, but we glory in our redemption. Come, precious Lord, to the Passover feast, and unite us as we stand in your presence.
(C) **AMEN.**

*Opening Hymn: "Beneath the Cross of Jesus"

WE STAND BEFORE THE CROSS

*(P) As we stand beneath the cross, let us make public confession to our God.

(C) **O SACRIFICIAL LAMB, I, A TROUBLED AND PENITENT SINNER, COME TO YOUR ABIDING PLACE, THE CROSS. I CONFESS TO YOU ALL MY SINS AND INIQUITIES WHICH HAVE SEPARATED ME FROM A RIGHT RELATIONSHIP WITH YOU. FOR THESE SINS I DESERVE DIVINE PUNISHMENT.**

BUT I AM TRULY SORRY FOR THEM, AND, REPENTING OF THEM, TURN TO YOU AND YOUR CROSS FOR FORGIVENESS AND MERCY.

FATHER, AS I LOOK UPON THE CROSS AND THE SUFFERING AND DEATH OF YOUR SON, JESUS CHRIST, BE GRACIOUS AND MERCIFUL TO ME, A SINNER.

FORGIVE MY SINS, CLEANSE ME IN CHRIST'S BLOOD, AND FILL ME WITH THY HOLY SPIRIT, THAT I MAY GO FORTH TO LIFE EVERLASTING. IN YOUR PRECIOUS NAME I PRAY. AMEN.

(P) The Almighty God in his mercy looks down upon us and through the sacrifice of Christ upon the Cross grants us forgiveness of our sins. In the name of the Father, the Son, and the Holy Spirit.

(C) **AMEN.**

THE LORD SPEAKS TO US ABOUT HIS CROSS

First Lesson: Ecclesiastes 9:1-6
Psalm 116:10-17 (read responsively)
Solo or Anthem
Gospel Lesson: Matthew 26:17-46
Meditation: "The Cross of Destiny"
Hymn

WE RESPOND TO THE CROSS
Prayers of the Church
Offering
Offertory
*Offertory Prayer

THE TABLE IS SPREAD BENEATH HIS CROSS
*The Great Thanksgiving
(P) The Lord be with you.
(C) **AND ALSO WITH YOU.**
(P) Lift up your hearts.
(C) **WE LIFT THEM TO THE LORD.**
(P) Let us give thanks to the Lord our God.
(C) **IT IS RIGHT TO GIVE HIM THANKS AND PRAISE.**
(P) It is indeed right and salutary that we should come to the feast of the Lamb this holy night. We join the celebration of remembrance of the first Passover instituted by God to remind his people of their deliverance. We approach the table now in remembrance of the last supper our Lord Jesus shared with his followers. We praise his name and join our voices in unending song.

*Sanctus
(C) **HOLY, HOLY, HOLY LORD, LORD GOD OF POWER AND MIGHT: HEAV'N AND EARTH ARE FULL OF YOUR GLORY. HOSANNA IN THE HIGHEST. BLESSED IS HE WHO COMES IN THE NAME OF THE LORD. HOSANNA IN THE HIGHEST.**

*Words of Institution
(P) Our Lord Jesus, on the night that he was betrayed, took bread, gave thanks, and broke it. Giving it to his disciples, he said, "Take and eat. This is my body, given for you. When you eat this, remember me." After the meal, he took the cup, gave thanks, and gave it to all to drink saying, "This cup is the new covenant in my blood, shed for you and for all people for the forgiveness of sin. When you drink it, remember me."

*Lord's Prayer
Distribution of Communion
(Communion hymns)
*Post Communion Prayer
(P) We give you thanks, O Lord, for the body and blood of Christ, which refreshes us with its healing power. As we have eaten and received of the sacrifice which he offered up for us upon the cross, send us forth tonight renewed in faith toward you and in increasing love toward one another. Through Jesus Christ our Lord.
(C) **AMEN.**

Stripping of the Altar (Congregation is seated)
Final Readings:
  Matthew 26:47-75 (Silence for reflection)
  Matthew 27:1-31 (Silence for reflection)

(No further words are said. The altar is stripped and the church is left in semi-darkness. All leave the church in silence, reflecting on the journey Christ now takes to the cross of destiny. Symbolically, Christ, stripped of his power and glory, is now in the hands of his captors but is fulfilling the will of the Father.)

***Congregation Stands**

THE CROSS OF DESTINY

Maundy Thursday

Lessons: Psalm 116 (10-17); Ecclesiastes 9:1-6; Matthew 26:17-46

We do a lot of preparing in life. We prepare meals in the home to meet our physical needs. We prepare our minds through education and training to meet our vocational goals. We prepare our hearts entering into relationships with family, friends, and that possible someone God has chosen for us to share our life with to meet our emotional desires. Much thought and careful planning go into each of these areas, but we should examine how much preparation goes into our spiritual lives as we approach the cross of destiny this Maundy Thursday night. As Christ's disciples prepared for the Passover, let us prepare to approach the cross once more. Let us pray:

Lord, on this night of remembrance, reveal our destiny and your will for our lives. As we celebrate the night in which you passed over the homes upon which blood was smeared, so pass over us who have received the blood of Christ as our salvation, so that we may not stand condemned before you on judgment day. Let us approach you knowing that you, Almighty God, are the one we are destined to see when death overtakes us. Fill us now with the love of Christ and guide us to life everlasting. In Jesus' name. Amen.

"Destiny" — the word itself stirs up within our spirits a feeling of being pulled along by an unseen power. Many of us feel we have no control over what our destiny may be and so simply drift along in life, buffeted by the waves that splash against our boats during the rough times, or peacefully relax in a pool of idleness at others. Whatever happens to come our way, we consider our "destiny" and sail on as we journey down the river of life. Others try to control their destinies by keeping a tight rein on their emotions, their pursuit of pleasure and wealth, their drive to move upward without regard to shady business deals or stepping on others to gain what they want. They are in control of the way their ship is moving and will not be pulled off course. They will not abandon themselves to what unbelievers call fate or to the outside source of power, called the Holy Spirit by believers, which may be guiding and directing their lives.

The writer of Ecclesiastes reminds us in our second reading that the good and the bad share the same destiny. Death is the common destiny of all human beings. The difference is in the way we approach our destiny. Those who believe in Jesus Christ are extended hope. They have become the "living" when they receive him as Lord and Savior. They pass from death to life. But those who have chosen to reject Jesus' invitation to come to the cross are doomed to a life of separation from God. They have no hope. Their rewards, which they accumulate here on earth, quickly vanish when confronted with their destiny, death. Their wills, which were never surrendered to Christ, now come face to face with what God's will was for them, to know Jesus and him crucified. God's plan for the salvation of the world did not exclude any person. He desires all to come to a saving knowledge of Christ, yet he gives his children the freedom to accept or reject their destiny.

Christ knew his destiny. He came into the world prepared to do his Father's will. Continually, he pulled apart to make sure that his will was lining up with God's. Communication with God through prayer enabled him to hear from God and to be strengthened to do what God was preparing him to do. His desert experience prepared him to enter a powerful three-year ministry as he walked the road to Jerusalem and to the cross which was his destiny.

The cross is also our destiny, and it is always ready, waiting for us in every place in our lives, for everything is reduced to the cross. We cannot escape it though we try. We are called, as Jesus was, to die on it. No matter where we try to steer our boats in life, we will meet the cross. It is not easy for us to crucify our flesh and our desires upon his cross. To bear the cross of Christ in suffering, to love the cross of Christ above all human loves, to bear the body and reduce it to servitude that we might purify the temple of the Spirit living within us, to flee from honors, to willingly suffer criticism and reproaches for his sake, to tolerate all adversities and losses, knowing that God is our all, to despise oneself that we may glorify only him, to be despised because of our decision to follow where he leads, and to not desire prosperity for ourself in this world, but to give that his kingdom would prosper, flies in the face of the cross and today's culture.

The world shouts, screams, even, at us to drink deeply of its chalice of pleasure, honor, prosperity, greed, license to do what makes one feel good, and achieve. Christ calls to us from the Passover table to drink from the cup of his blood poured out for many for the forgiveness of sins. The cup the world offers brings only temporary consolation. The momentary quenching of the thirst is quickly gone. As we take and eat the body of Christ which he offered on that cross and drink from the cup of heavenly consolation, we receive our destiny as children of God. Christ was prepared to drink the cup of suffering which awaited him upon the cross. In the garden he sought his Father's will again in this matter, asking that if possible, the cup would be removed. Yet he prayed not what he wanted, but what God wanted be done. This surrendering of his will to the ultimate will of the Father was not easy. Christ knows how difficult it is for each of us to deliberately choose his will and not our own. "The sorrow in my heart is so great that it almost crushes me," he told the disciples as he asked them to stay and watch with him. He left to be with God and agonize over his destiny. He called upon the unseen power, that outside source which guides and directs our lives, that the course might just be changed. But it was that surrender to the will of the Father that enabled him to leave the garden in peace and walk the road to Calvary.

Death is that common destiny we all share. We are on a path to death from the moment we are born, just as Christ was. His life was filled with the knowledge of what he had been sent to do, redeem a lost and sinful world. As God prepared him to face the cross, so God is at work in each of us to bring us to the point of surrendering our wills to him. Our crucifixion awaits us. Will we die that we might have life?

As you come to the Lord's table and share in the celebration of that last supper, come to your death. Eat the bread, his flesh which endured the pain and humiliation of such a painful death. Drink the cup, his blood poured out so that you may be washed clean from your sin. Come and face your destiny now. Jesus calls to each of us to head our boats into the harbor of his cross. For it is inevitable that we face that cross, for God has ordained it. In his name, Amen.

THE MÁNY-SIDED CROSS
GOOD FRIDÁY OBSERVÁNCE

Prelude

WE VIEW THE CROSS FROM A DISTANCE

*(P) Lord, we stand on this side of the cross knowing what lies ahead for you this day. As you were led out to be crucified, Almighty God, lead us back in time to Calvary that we might stand before you aware of our sinfulness;

(C) **SIN DARKENS OUR SOULS. HAVE MERCY, O LORD.**

(P) As we journeyed with you from the festive Passover meal, O Lord, we entered the garden of struggle;

(C) **SEE OUR STRUGGLES TO BE FREED FROM SIN.**

(P) Forgive us for letting our spirits sleep at times as did your disciples that night.

(C) **AWAKEN US NOW TO YOUR SUFFERING.**

(P) Not what you willed, you prayed, but what God willed be done;

(C) **YOUR WILL BE DONE IN OUR LIVES.**

(P) We stand with Peter denying you at times;

(C) **GIVE US STRENGTH TO DAILY PROFESS YOU.**

(P) Take our hand in your nail-pierced hands and lead us along on this journey;

(C) **WE ARE AWARE OF YOUR WOUNDS. NOW OPEN OUR EARS TO YOUR CRIES.**

*Opening Hymn

WE PRAISE THE CROSS OF CHRIST

*(P) Father, you sent your Son to die for us;
(C) **WE PRAISE YOUR PLAN OF SALVATION.**
(P) The cross now stands before our eyes;
(C) **WE PRAISE YOUR PLAN OF SALVATION.**

(P) We see ourselves as wrapped in sin;
(C) **WE PRAISE YOUR PLAN OF SALVATION.**
(P) You took the burden of our sin upon that cross;
(C) **WE PRAISE YOUR PLAN OF SALVATION.**
(P) Reach out, O Christ, with your wounded hands;
(C) **WE PRAISE YOUR PLAN OF SALVATION.**
(P) And heal our spirits through your blood;
(C) **WE PRAISE YOUR PLAN OF SALVATION.**

Anthem

THE WORD SPEAKS OF CHRIST'S SUFFERINGS

First Reading: Isaiah 52:13—53:12
(Silence for reflection)
Psalm 22:1-23
(Read responsively)
Second Reading: Matthew 27:1-31
(Silence for reflection)
Hymn
Gospel Reading: Matthew 27:32-66
(Silence for reflection)
Meditation: "The Cross of Commitment"
(Silence for reflection)

THE SIDES OF THE CROSS SPEAK

*(P) Hear Jesus' words from the cross: "Father forgive them; for they know not what they do."
(C) **WE EMBRACE THE CROSS OF REPENTANCE.**
(P) Hear Jesus' words from the cross: "Truly, I say to you, today you will be with me in paradise."
(C) **WE EMBRACE THE CROSS OF HOPE.**
(P) Hear Jesus' words from the cross: "Woman, behold your son! Behold, your mother."
(C) **WE EMBRACE THE CROSS OF LOVE.**

(P) Hear Jesus' words from the cross: "My God, my God, why hast thou forsaken me?"
(C) **WE EMBRACE THE CROSS OF MYSTERY.**
(P) Hear Jesus' words from the cross: "I thirst."
(C) **WE EMBRACE THE CROSS OF FREEDOM.**
(P) Hear Jesus' words from the cross: "It is finished."
(C) **WE EMBRACE THE CROSS OF LIFE.**
(P) We are all destined to die.
(C) **WE EMBRACE THE CROSS OF DESTINY.**
(P) May we choose today to die with Christ.
(C) **WE EMBRACE THE CROSS OF COMMITMENT.**

WE PRAY TO THE CROSS

*(P) Lord Jesus, look with mercy upon us today. We see the nails which pierce your feet and hands. We see the stripes of your beatings upon your flesh. The crown of thorns which encircles your brow is tinged with your dried blood. You hang before us stripped of your clothing. Naked we stand before you. The insults and jeers which are hurled toward your cross ring in our ears, causing tears to stain our face. Your agony is so real as you hang before us. "It is finished," you cry and so are released from this life. Release us, now O Lord, as we embrace your cross, for truly today we see and feel the love you have for us. For Christ's sake we pray.
(C) **AMEN.**

*Lord's Prayer

Solo: "Were You There When They Crucified My Lord?"

(Shroud may then be draped on the cross and a rose placed on the altar. The Christ candle is then extinguished. Lights dimmed.)

(P) As the light has gone out of the world, we enter a period of darkness. Christ is dead. His body lies in a tomb. You are welcome to remain and reflect upon God's love for you in Jesus' sufferings and death as you embrace the cross. Please leave in silence.

(All leave in silence.)

***Congregation Stands**

THE CROSS OF COMMITMENT

Good Friday

Lessons: Psalm 22:1-23; Isaiah 52:13—53:12; Matthew 27:1-65

Driving down a turnpike in a strange city can be a traumatic experience for many of us. We rely on the road signs to give us proper warning of when we need to switch lanes in order to make the proper turn. Heaven forbid if a semi gets in front of us and blocks our view! All of a sudden, we need to cross over to the turning lane, and we just happen to have been cruising in the fast lane. Stress mounts as we feel the crunch of the cars around us refusing to give us entry into their lane. Everyone's on their own course and not really interested in being courteous to a "stranger" in their midst. Horns honk, and fists are raised. You can just hear them mutter, "Darn out-of-state driver!" Crossing over those five lanes and turning toward the freedom of the off ramp and your correct destiny down the highway, you exit at the next rest stop to pull your frazzled nerves together and regroup, making a deliberate pause to take out the map and find out exactly where you are and how far you need to travel to get to your ultimate destination.

That's what Good Friday can be for us, a rest stop in our journey down the road of life. Everyone feels life is speeding along too fast. Things seem out of control as we are bombarded with personal time crunches, financial struggles, health and family issues, as well as upheavals on all fronts in our world. Certainly we don't need to be confronted in our faith. But that is what Good Friday and the cross do: confront! Some people refuse to stop at this day. They enter Jerusalem with Christ in triumph on Palm Sunday, may pause at the communion rail on Maundy Thursday in reverence, but then pass by the suffering of Good Friday because it makes them feel too uncomfortable, and exit on Easter Day in glorious celebration, feeling good about our "religious observations." For some it may simply be putting in time, coming to worship an impersonal God and bowing our heads, grateful for the pause but then hurriedly rushing off to do the next thing on our busy agendas. We need to avoid those semis which obscure our view and block the road signs which keep us in the right lane headed toward Jesus. God plants the cross and Good Friday squarely on our turnpike of life so that we will collide with them. They are not to be avoided. God wants us to die on impact in order for his Son to reach out from that cross and give us life again. Yet how many of us are committed to the wrong lane? How many of us are committed to living out our life our way apart from Jesus? How many of us are committed to dying?

Jesus was committed to doing his Father's will. He was not excited about what lay before him as he struggled in prayer, asking God to take away the cup of suffering which he would have to drink from at the cross. But he committed himself to doing what God desired, not avoiding the path that would lead to the cross, but deliberately setting his eyes on the road straight ahead.

Jesus encountered many along the path to the cross who would wrestle with the cross of commitment which now confronted them. The first were his own disciples, who fell asleep at the wheel of prayer. Their spirits were willing, but they gave into the flesh and fell asleep. When the soldiers came to arrest their leader, they became frightened about what their own fates would be and leaped by their vehicle, leaving Christ alone at the wheel. The shepherd watched with understanding eyes as his flock took flight. Commitment was there in the good times, but when the rubber hit the road, even Peter, who had adamantly committed to follow wherever Jesus would lead, had a blow out. Colliding with the cross, these men found out exactly how shaky their commitment to Christ actually was.

Christ is a person. Christ is not a cause. We need to watch that we don't just come to church to earn a gold star on the roster in heaven and do "good" things like reach out to the poor, love our neighbor, feed the hungry, write letters of protest over racism, sanctions, etc. to earn God's approval. Causes may become semis which divert our attention from the true focus of our faith, Jesus the suffering servant, the sacrifice for sin. Judas followed a cause. As a zealot, he wanted Jesus to be committed to the overthrow of the foreign government which oppressed his nation. Hoping to spur Christ on to being the military Messiah who would overthrow Roman rule, he betrayed him. As a follower of Christ, he had misread the road signs. Realizing that Christ was committed to a different course of action and now stood condemned, he suffered great remorse. The cause now disappeared in light of the reality of what would now happen to the person of Christ. The cross of Good Friday, the cross of commitment, plunged him into such deep despair that he took his own life.

Those Christ stood before — his captors — were committed to religion. The learned teachers of the law, the chief priests and elders who carried out the task of worship, making sure it was done properly, even the High Priest himself, all had their vision blurred and missed God standing in their midst. They refused to move out of their lane of travel as Christ directed them to another path. How many today fail to hear God's voice calling to them to turn from their collision course with sin and embrace the cross? The followers of God that Christ stood before were committed to a system. Are we committed to a system called church or to the person who hung on that cross, committed to the work of saving our souls?

Pilate was committed to keeping peace. Jesus was a stumbling block along his path. This person had stirred up the people he governed with all those reported miracles and now the "religious," who would rather see Pilate ousted, had deliberately sent Jesus to him, forcing him to make a decision. Try as he might to get rid of dealing with Christ, he was forced to face him. Pilate, however, when offered a chance to change the course of his life, chose to stay right where he was, not detour or listen to the warnings of his wife who claimed Christ innocent. The Prince of Peace stood squarely before him, forcing him to make a commitment to a course of action, but he passed the buck to the crowd. They would make the decision about the direction of this man's fate. "Crucify him!" they cried. "Let his blood be on us and on our children." They plunged headlong into the guard rails, avoiding the cross Jesus asked them to embrace.

We might ask if there were any along the path to Calvary who were committed to Christ? Simon, the man forced to take on Christ's cross, did so unwillingly. He was given no choice. Those Jesus encountered before that time had that option. There will come a time for each of us at death, when we will discover the cost of our free choice. God offers us the choice to accept or reject our Lord. He desires for us to do so willingly, not out of fear of punishment, but out of love for what his Son did on the cross so that we might escape our punishment.

Two viewed the commitment of Christ in carrying out his Father's will as they hung with him on their individual crosses. One wanted Christ to release him from his present sufferings. Many turn to Jesus in the hard times for rescue, as one awaiting a divine ambulance. Yet they will then ignore the call of the cross when it becomes an intrusion on lifestyle, time, finances, and a call to commitment. Committed to his own welfare, the one robber could not throw himself upon the mercy of God in repentance. He sealed his fate by his rejection of the Son of Man. The other realized his sinfulness, turned to the cross, and committed his fate to Christ. He had seen in Jesus an opening to a new lane. He desired to pull over and was offered the opportunity to pass from death to life.

The women who stood beneath the cross were committed. They made public profession of their faith by clinging to the cross and their Lord. Joseph of Arimathea, the disciple of the dark, now stepped out into the light, showing his commitment and risking his reputation by claiming the body of Christ. We need to stand up for Christ in all areas of our lives. We need to let the life of Jesus shine forth in all we do.

We need to examine our commitment to Jesus. As we encounter the cross of Christ on the highways of our lives, will we swerve to avoid it as the Pharisees and Sadducees did? Will we avoid a personal relationship with Jesus in favor of a social relationship with him?

Look up! Do we see the cross approaching? What will our reaction be to that collision course we are destined to have with it? Do we need to be awakened as the disciples were who fell asleep at the wheel? Will we flee from the cross because we fear Christ might ask too much of us? Will we rush to embrace causes and divert our attention from forming a personal relationship with our loving Lord? Have we misread the road signs because we neglect to learn of Christ through prayer and his Word? Do we ignore the voice which calls to us to turn from sin? Are we so entrenched in our "system" that we miss the reality of Jesus in our lives? Have we passed the buck, given someone else the token to carry out God's work here on earth? Have we purposefully decided to reject Christ and commit spiritual suicide? Have we put Christ's interests ahead of our own, passing smoothly from one lane to the next under his direction? Will we willingly embrace the cross, planting ourselves firmly beneath it so all will see we are committed to a living Lord? Will we give public witness to our faith in Jesus?

Good Friday and the cross are here, calling us to pull off the busy road of our lives for reflection. Have you read the road signs correctly? Is your destination Jesus? Are you in the right lane to pass over from death to life? Pull up at the cross and examine your commitment to Christ. Gaze upon the one who conquered death and calls on you to die so that you may truly live. Aim yourself directly at his cross and collide with it head on today. Commit yourself to die so that you may truly live. In Christ's name we pray. Amen.

THE MANY-SIDED CROSS
EASTER VIGIL

WILL YOU TARRY WITH THE LORD THIS NIGHT?

*(P) We enter the darkness of this Easter vigil in the hope of encountering the light of Christ Jesus our Lord. Will you tarry with the Lord this night?

Silence for Reflection

A NIGHT OF EXAMINATION

*(P) On the night our Lord Jesus was betrayed, he entered the garden to pray. Turning to his disciples he admonished them, "Pray that you will not fall into temptation." Then he withdrew to be with his Father in prayer.

(C) **FORGIVE US, LORD, FOR BEING TEMPTED TO NOT DRAW INTO YOUR PRESENCE.**

(P) Jesus prayed that the cup of suffering would be taken from him, but not his will but the Father's be done.

(C) **FORGIVE US, LORD, FOR BEING TEMPTED TO SEEK OUR OWN WILL AND NOT YOURS.**

(P) Strengthened by an angel, Christ prayed earnestly. His sweat fell like blood to the ground.

(C) **FORGIVE US, LORD, FOR NOT EXERTING OURSELVES IN PRAYER.**

(P) Jesus returned to the disciples, only to find them asleep.

(C) **FORGIVE US, LORD, FOR NOT BEING ABLE TO TARRY WITH YOU IN YOUR HOUR OF PRAYER.**

(P) The betrayer came and kissed him.

(C) **FORGIVE US, LORD, FOR THE MANY BETRAYALS IN OUR LIVES AND OUR QUICK EMBRACES WITH THE WORLD INSTEAD OF YOU.**

(P) Soldiers seized our Lord and led him away. He was denied by his own, mocked and beaten by unbelievers, tried without justice, not recognized by those he came to save, sentenced by his governing body, and crucified with criminals.

(C) **FORGIVE US, LORD, FOR THE TIMES WE HAVE MOCKED AND DENIED YOU IN OUR OWN LIVES.**
(P) On that Black Friday, one man died to sin by turning to you; one man died in sin by thinking only of himself; but one Man died specifically for sin to gain eternal life for all.
(C) **FORGIVE US, LORD, FOR CENTERING ON OURSELVES AND NOT LOOKING TO YOU AS YOU SUFFERED ON THAT CROSS FOR US.**
(P) The angel of death descended, and Christ gave his spirit up to him.
(C) **FORGIVE US, LORD, FOR FEARING DEATH. HELP US TO COMMIT THAT TIME TO YOU.**
(P) Those who watched began to understand the depth of love he had for others.
(C) **FORGIVE US, LORD, FOR NOT RECOGNIZING YOUR LOVE.**
ALL: HELP US TARRY WITH YOU THIS NIGHT, DEAR LORD.

A NIGHT OF WAITING

Light one candle.
(P) We light our first candle in the name of the Father.

Hymn: "Go to Dark Gethsemane" (vs. 1, 2, 3)

(P) The soldiers around the cross waited for the three to die. The Jews waited for their deaths to be hurried along to meet the requirements of the law.
(C) **LORD, WE AWAIT FREEDOM FROM THE LAW OF SIN AND DEATH.**
(P) Your side, O Lord, was pierced; your bones were broken.
(C) **LORD, WE AWAIT THE PIERCING OF OUR HEARTS AND THE BROKENNESS OF OUR PRIDE.**
(P) Joseph of Arimathea was a man waiting for the Kingdom of God.
(C) **LORD, WE AWAIT YOUR RESURRECTION.**

(P) Nicodemus had been told, "You must be born again!"
(C) **LORD, WE AWAIT NEW BIRTH THROUGH YOUR SPIRIT.**
(P) The two took your body, prepared it, and laid it in the empty tomb in the garden.
(C) **LORD, PREPARE US TO BE LAID IN THE TOMB. WE AWAIT OUR DEATH TO SELF.**
(P) Your followers observed the letter of the law and waited on the Sabbath behind the closed doors.
(C) **LORD, WE AWAIT THE OPENING OF THE DOORS OF OUR HEARTS.**
(P) Wrapped in grief, they thought only of the grave. Their hopes were buried with their friend.
(C) **LORD, WE AWAIT YOU IN THIS NIGHT.**
ALL: **HELP US O TARRY WITH YOU THIS NIGHT, DEAR LORD.**

A NIGHT OF LEARNING

Light second candle.

(P) We light our second candle in the name of the Son.

Hymn: "All Praise to Thee, My God, This Night"

Meditation: "Crossroads"

THE NIGHT ENDS

Light third candle.

(P) We light our third candle in the name of the Spirit.

Hymn: "That Easter Day with Joy Was Bright"

(P) We have tarried with our Lord through this Easter vigil. We see the first light of dawn that signals the night's end. We run with Mary and are met with an open tomb. Angels greet us with the news that he is not here. "He is risen!"

(C) **LORD, WE SEEK YOU AMONG THE DEAD. TURN OUR EYES FROM THE NIGHT TO THE LIGHT OF DAY.**
(P) Mary wept. She could not find him. The Light stood before her, and then she knew.
(C) **LORD, WE TURN TO THE LIGHT AND RECOGNIZE YOU AS OUR RISEN LORD.**
(P) "I have seen the Lord," she reports to the others.
(C) **LORD, TONIGHT WE SEE YOU!**
ALL: **LORD, WE WANT TO TARRY WITH YOU FOREVER!**

A NEW DAY BEGINS

*Hymn: "Jesus Christ is Risen Today!"

*(P) We come to your table, Lord, to be refreshed from the darkness of the grave watch. Flood us with the remembrance of your new covenant as we share the sacred elements.
(C) **WE SEEK TO BE RENEWED THROUGH YOUR BODY AND BLOOD.**
(P) Come and share in his resurrection.
(C) **RISEN LORD, WE COME.**

Communion

HE WILL NOT TARRY

*(P) Our Lord's body and blood strengthen you as you await his coming again.
(C) **LORD JESUS, COME SOON. WE ASK YOU NOT TO TARRY LONG.**
(P) Hear the Lord's words from the book of Revelation.

Revelation 22:16-17, 20:

"I, Jesus, have sent my angel to give you this testimony for the churches. I am the Root and the Offspring of David, and the bright Morning Star."

The Spirit and the bride say, "Come!" And let him who hears say, "Come!" Whoever is thirsty, let him come; and whoever wishes, let him take the free gift of the water of life. He who testifies to these things says, "Yes, I am coming soon!"
(C) **AMEN. COME, LORD JESUS. COME SOON!**

*Hymn: "Come Thou Almighty King"

*Congregation Stands

CROSSROADS

Easter Vigil

Text: Luke 23:50-55

Have you ever gone for a Sunday drive in unfamiliar territory and suddenly found yourself at a crossroads, not knowing which way to turn? You know the road you have just travelled down, but now you are unsure of which route to take to reach your destination. The choice you make will impact your schedule. You will eventually reach your destination, but if the wrong choice is made, it could take longer to arrive. We stand tonight at a crossroads in our journey through Holy Week. We know where we have been, for we look to the darkness of Good Friday. We know where we are going, for tomorrow we celebrate the resurrection of our Lord. We know for a fact that Jesus Christ died, was buried, and rose again. Our anticipation of tomorrow's blessed event is filled with joy. Songs of praise will rise from our lips — Jesus Christ is risen! Alleluia! But as we sit and await this event, we should become aware of the fact that God places each of us at a crossroads of faith between Good Friday and Easter morning. He places before us the good news of the death and resurrection of his Son and then awaits our response. We need to pass through the vigil of Easter, the time of waiting from the crucifixion until the resurrection. We need to stand at the crossroads and ponder the route we will take in our walk with Christ.

The followers of Jesus were unaware that they stood at a crossroads. They saw the cross as a dead end. Those who stood at the foot of the cross were engulfed in an atmosphere of grief and despair. Drained of all emotion, those who witnessed the crucifixion felt all hope dashed as they witnessed Christ breathe his last breath and cry out, "It is finished!" They waited to tend the Lord's dead body. The other two had not yet died, and the Sabbath was approaching fast. The soldiers broke the legs of the two criminals to speed their deaths, but when they came to Jesus and saw that he was already dead, they pierced his side, bringing forth a flow of blood and water. Truly, it was finished.

"It is finished!" These words might have been uttered by another as he rolled a stone against the door of the tomb. Joseph of Arimathea performed the last sad motions of winding up the whole affair — a sad finality to such a promising future.

Joseph of Arimathea has often been referred to as a "twilight disciple" or the "disciple of the dark." The foundation for this reputation is based on the fact that he did nothing until after Jesus was dead, and then not until darkness had fallen. This is an unfair description for one of the more powerful members of the Sanhedrin.

We know from Scripture that Joseph was a very rich and highly respected member of the council. He had come from a tiny village in the northwest corner of central Judea, from the hillsides of Arimathea. His wealth was probably amassed after his move to Jerusalem, for the unused tomb he had in his possession was new. If he had been of an old aristocratic family, he would have had a family tomb. Of course, since Jewish law prohibited burying executed criminals in family tombs, it may have been necessary to use a special tomb. Even so, for Joseph to have possessed an extra tomb is a sign of affluence. He also associated with those of wealth. John tells us that he was not alone in burying the body of Jesus. "He was accompanied by Nicodemus, the man who earlier had visited Jesus at night. Nicodemus brought a mixture of myrrh and aloes, about seventy-five pounds." Nicodemus had provided at his own considerable expense the spices for the preparation of the body. But is it the wealth of Joseph that makes this man an object of our reflection tonight?

Mark's account of the burial tells us that Joseph was a man "looking for the kingdom of God." This in itself could mean nothing more than that he was a good Pharisee. Since he took seriously the rabbinic tradition that a dead body should not be allowed to remain unburied beyond the day of death, he might just have been performing an act of piety by removing the body of Jesus and burying it, but Joseph had come to a crossroads in his life. The Gospel of Mark gives us more information about the choice he had to make concerning the inner conflict which must have been occurring in this man.

Joseph took courage and went to Pilate. The man who had been brought this King of the Jews and who tried to release him now was approached by one of those who belonged to the ruling body that had demanded his death. How this must have puzzled the governor. It took a great deal of courage for Joseph to face Pilate and risk official disapproval. It took even more courage and determination to face those of his countrymen who had engineered the crime of Christ's crucifixion. We do not know exactly how Joseph first heard about Jesus. Perhaps he met him during the last week in Jerusalem. Maybe he had heard Jesus preach or had seen the many miracles that he had performed. He could have been influenced during Jesus' trial, for Luke points out that Joseph was unsympathetic with the intent of the council and refused to give his consent to the action that the Sanhedrin took in condemning Jesus.

Joseph stood at a crossroads because he was a man "looking for the kingdom of God." He chose to seek Pilate's permission to claim the body and bury it. He chose to give Jesus a decent burial. In his search for the Kingdom of God, Joseph had encountered its king. Scripture tells us that "those who seek God will find him." In this seeking, Joseph had unknowingly been given a special gift by God: the responsibility of caring for the body of his own beloved Son. To Joseph, however, his seeking seemed to have come to an end in despair and sadness. As he carried the body of Christ to the tomb hewn out of solid rock, in a garden not far from the scene of the crucifixion, he must have looked upon the lifeless body of Jesus and mourned. As he wrapped the body in linen strips, he must have wrapped the last hopes of his search along with it. The silence that must have surrounded him and Nicodemus did not dispel the unanswered questions. Rolling the stone in front of the door of the tomb, Joseph must have given a sigh of despair. It was finished. Jesus Christ lay dead in that tomb. What more could he do? The soldiers who now took up their duty as sentries over the grave were a stern reminder that Caesar's kingdom still ruled. He turned in silence with his friend and returned home to grieve in privacy behind closed doors.

But God showed Joseph the gift he had in mind for the whole world from the beginning of time. All the world stood at a crossroads that night. Jesus was dead, but he would not remain dead. God raised his Son from death. Jesus did not need that tomb, and neither would Joseph of Arimathea, whose faith in Jesus Christ had brought him into the kingdom. Joseph found what he was seeking, the gift of God, eternal life through Jesus Christ our Lord.

Joseph looked at the roads which lay before him that Good Friday. He saw the road that Jesus had travelled on his way to the cross. Joseph could have chosen to walk away from the cross, to live his life apart from his knowledge of who this Jesus was. But Joseph chose to walk with his Lord, even though that One was now dead. He followed a higher impulse that would see to the proper burial for a beloved leader. He chose to risk incurring the wrath of his peers by seeking Pilate's permission to bury Christ. He chose the right path and was rewarded with going down in biblical record as a man who cared for our dear Lord.

Joseph walked away from a dead Lord. On the morrow he would hear the news of a living Lord. Tonight you stand at a crossroads in this Easter vigil. Will you turn from the tomb and remember a dead Lord, or will you walk forth tonight knowing that your Lord lives? Have you come here tonight looking for the kingdom of God, as Joseph did? If so, respond as he did and seek God. Seek him with your whole heart, but don't look into a tomb, for the stone which Joseph placed in front of it did not keep Christ entombed. God rolled the stone away! He opened a closed tomb and can open the closed tombs of our hearts. Do not seek Christ among the dead, for he is alive! He lives! He has risen! Risen to bring all who believe in him eternal life!

As you stand at the crossroads tonight, consider the route you will choose to bring you closer to your destination: eternal life with Jesus Christ. Embrace the living Lord and proclaim with the company of believers on Easter Day, "Christ our Lord is risen today. Alleluia!" Amen.

THE MANY-SIDED CROSS
EASTER SUNRISE SERVICE

Prelude

GOD ENTERS OUR WORSHIP

*(P) Let us rise and hear the Word of God proclaimed from the Psalms. Give thanks to the Lord for he is good;
(C) **His love endures forever.**
(P) Let Israel say:
(C) **HIS LOVE ENDURES FOREVER.**
(P) Shouts of joy and victory resound in the tents of the righteous.
(C) **THE LORD'S RIGHT HAND HAS DONE MIGHTY THINGS!**
(P) The Lord's right hand is lifted high;
(C) **THE LORD'S RIGHT HAND HAS DONE MIGHTY THINGS!**
(P) I will not die but live,
(C) **AND WILL PROCLAIM WHAT THE LORD HAS DONE.**
(P) The Lord has chastened me severely,
(C) **BUT HE HAS NOT GIVEN ME OVER TO DEATH.**
(P) Open for me the gates of righteousness;
(C) **I WILL ENTER AND GIVE THANKS TO THE LORD.**
(P) This is the gate of the Lord through which the righteous may enter;
(C) **I WILL GIVE THANKS, FOR YOU HAVE ANSWERED ME; YOU HAVE BECOME MY SALVATION.**
(P) The stone which the builders rejected has become the capstone;
(C) **THE LORD HAS DONE THIS, AND IT IS MARVELOUS IN OUR EYES.**
(P) This is the day the Lord has made;
(C) **LET US REJOICE AND BE GLAD IN IT!**

CHRIST ENTERS OUR WORSHIP

*Christ candle enters from the back of the church.
(P) Alleluia! Christ has risen!
(C) **HE IS RISEN INDEED!**
(P) The grave is empty. We are free!
(C) **HE IS RISEN INDEED!**
(P) Rejoice and shout the victory,
(C) **HE IS RISEN INDEED!**

*Processional Hymn

*Invocation:
(P) O Risen Lord, the gates of death have opened wide announcing your victory. Come into our worship now, Almighty God, as we behold the Risen Christ. With shouts of joy we praise the Rock upon whom your church is built. Be present now, O God of Love, as we greet you this happy Easter morn.
(C) **ALLELUIA! CHRIST IS PRESENT! HE IS RISEN INDEED!**

THE WORD ENTERS OUR WORSHIP

*Prayer of the Day:
(P) The Lord be with you.
(C) **AND ALSO WITH YOU.**
(P) Let us pray: Creator God, as you spoke the Word, light broke into the darkness, and Creation rejoiced that blessed day. As you became the Word in Jesus who dwelt among us, Creation again sang your praises. As You fulfilled your Word in your death and resurrection, Creation rejoiced that Easter morn. Be with us now through the Word and Spirit as we rejoice in our life of faith.
(C) **AMEN.**

First Lesson: Isaiah 25:6-9
Anthem
Second Lesson: 1 Corinthians 15:19-28
*Alleluia
*Gospel: John 20:1-9 (10-18)
Easter Message: "What's On Your Easter Menu?"
Easter Hymn

WE RESPOND AS EASTER PEOPLE

*Our Confession of Sin
  (P) We stand before the Risen Christ and confess our sin in order to obtain his forgiveness.
  (C) **LORD, WE ARE UNWORTHY TO APPROACH YOU IN A SINFUL STATE. WE CONFESS UNTO YOU OUR UNBELIEF, OUR WAYWARDNESS, OUR MISGUIDED ZEAL. LOOK WITH FAVOR UPON US, YOUR CHOSEN PEOPLE, AND THROUGH THE BLOOD OF CHRIST POURED OUT UPON THE CROSS, CLEANSE US FROM ALL SIN SO WE MAY GO FORTH FORGIVEN, PROCLAIMING DAILY YOUR DEATH AND RESURRECTION AS GLORIOUS EASTER PEOPLE. AMEN.**

*Our Confession of Faith
  (P) As believers on this side of the cross, we have become an Easter people. Let us then confess our faith in the Risen Christ.
*Apostles' Creed
*Prayers of The Church
Our Confession Through Action
Offering
*Offertory
*(P) Receive the gifts we offer up, O Risen Lord, that the message of this Easter Day would be proclaimed throughout the world. To this end we pray.
  (C) **AMEN.**

THE RISEN CHRIST CONFRONTS US IN SACRAMENT

*The Great Thanksgiving
*Sanctus
*Words of Institution
*Lord's Prayer
*(P) God has prepared a feast for all people through the body and blood of our Lord Jesus Christ. Join us now as we remember again that sacrifice through this blessed sacrament.
  Distribution of Communion
  Communion Hymns

THE RISEN CHRIST GOES FORTH IN JOY

*Easter Litany
  (P) Having feasted at the table of our Lord,
  (C) **WE GO FORTH WITH HIM RENEWED.**
  (P) God has prepared us anew to go forth in joy strengthened through his body and blood.
  (C) **WE GO FORTH WITH HIM RENEWED.**
  (P) The shroud which wrapped us so tightly is now loosed.
  (C) **WE GO FORTH WITH HIM RENEWED.**
  (P) "The tomb is empty!" we thus proclaim.
  (C) **WE GO FORTH WITH HIM RENEWED.**
  (P) Sing praises to our God and King!
  (C) **WE GO FORTH WITH HIM RENEWED.**

*Easter Benediction
  (C) **As the good news was spread that Easter morn, receive it and God's benediction: Go forth in joy and proclaim God's love from the Father through the Son and by the Holy Spirit. Amen.**
  (C) **JESUS CHRIST IS RISEN TODAY. GLORY ALLELUIA!**
*Recessional Hymn
*Congregation Stands

WHAT'S ON YOUR EASTER MENU?

Easter Sunrise

Lessons: Psalm 118:1-2, 15-24; Isaiah 25:6-9;
1 Corinthians 15:19-28; John 20:1-9 (10-18)

Alleluia! Christ has risen, the tomb is empty, He is free! Alleluia! Easter has arrived! Christ has brought us a new menu for life: he has brought us an "Easter Menu."

Many today will visit their grandparents following church for an Easter breakfast of pancakes and sausage. A number of dads might opt to treat the family to an Egg McMuffin under the golden arches. Some may even have reservations for a brunch of ham, chicken, and assorted goodies at a local restaurant. For others it may be a quiet meal of one sunny-side-up egg and a piece of toast and jam in their own kitchens. Around the country, a lot of church folk turn out to support their youth on Easter morn, hard youth workers and advisors serving an Easter menu of scrambled eggs, French toast, and homemade coffee cakes. Wherever you may have decided to feast, the menu for Easter breakfast will hopefully fill you and make your day special. But there is an Easter menu prepared for us that will truly fill. Jesus Christ has provided a menu for Easter which fills the hearts of believers everywhere, making Easter Day a special occasion.

Mary Magdalene entered the garden that first Easter morning with an empty heart. The feasts she had enjoyed with Christ were now over. Her Lord was dead. Mary had seen his body broken upon the cross in death. The world had served her a menu of tears, heartbreak, and hopelessness. But Christ had an Easter menu awaiting this faithful follower. She had come to the tomb expecting a dead Jesus, and instead found a living Lord. She stood before the Risen Lord: Jesus not broken and bleeding, drained of life, but Jesus filled with abundant, radiant life.

We come to church on Easter morning to celebrate that resurrection. As believers in the resurrection, we serve and worship a living Christ. Our God is not dead; he is alive! We have proof served to us as the first course on our Easter menu: the real, physical presence of Christ in the garden and in our hearts.

Our Easter menu continues. Christ looked upon the weeping Mary with love, taking the tears flowing from a broken heart and changing them into tears of joy. Mary wept for Jesus as she saw him crucified, and then she wept for herself. The one who had offered her forgiveness and love was no longer there to extend his friendship. To be in his presence brought her security and joy. Now that security was gone. She could not turn to the disciples for protection. They had fled at his arrest and were hiding out in fear for their own lives. What sort of protection could they offer her? Her joy had turned to despair. What was to become of her now?

But Christ served Mary and serves us a new entree: a personal relationship with him. Jesus wept. He loved his friends and cried over their deaths. He loved Jerusalem and wept over her condition. He experienced tears in his life as many disappointed him. So as he takes our tears and mixes them with his own, he offers back the reality of his presence with us in all circumstances. Sickness, suffering, family strife, death, all bring tears to our eyes as we weep over the condition of our world and those we live in community with. But Christ took all of that upon his body at Calvary. He clears our eyes so that we can see his real presence. But, like Mary, we need to be looking for the Lord. Jesus asked Mary, "Woman, why are you crying? Who is it you are looking for?" In this world there will be many things which cause us to weep, but Christ promises that he will be with us. He will wipe away our tears, replacing them with his comfort.

The next item on the Easter menu Jesus serves is that of action. The disciples had locked themselves away in fear following Christ's arrest, but the news that Mary brought them that Easter morning shook them out of their despair and prompted them to action. "They have taken the Lord out of the tomb, and we don't know where they have put him." Immediately the disciples were moved to act upon her words. Running to the tomb, they left their fear behind, expecting to confront the body snatchers. What greeted them was more than they could understand at the moment. The tomb was open, the linen strips and burial cloth neatly folded, and the body gone. No signs of foul play, but signs of a God who had taken action by raising his Son from the dead, just as he said he would. They saw and believed, but still did not understand. Christ challenges us with this item on his Easter menu to do likewise. Come to the tomb. The stone was rolled away, not to let Jesus out, but to allow us to look in and believe. Then go forth in action to announce the glorious news of Easter Day, "He is risen."

Christ next offers up another wonderful course for us to enjoy: freedom. When Christ raised Lazarus from the dead, Lazarus emerged from the tomb in the bondage of the grave clothes. But when God raised Jesus from the dead, the grave clothes were freed from body. We are freed from the bondage of sin and death through Christ's death and glorious resurrection. Those sins which seek to keep us tied up have been forgiven. We have freedom from sin and are set free to announce that to others. We do not wander around this world like mummies, wrapped tightly in bondage, for Jesus Christ has released us. "If the Son has set you free, you are free indeed." We are free as we turn from our sin, embrace the cross, die to self, and then are raised to new life in Christ — free to be the person Christ has called us to be in him, whole and liberated. Jesus secures us the freedom to choose.

Finally, Christ presents the final course on our Easter menu: hope of eternal life. This is a dessert item, for even if there were no eternal life offered, we would have full stomachs by simply ingesting the first courses. The reality of a living Lord, whose body was broken and whose blood was shed for each of us, makes us grateful. The knowledge that the tears we shed have been shed by a loving Father as he watched the death of his Son enables us to look upon others with compassion and to receive comfort in our times of grief. The faith which the Spirit implants in our hearts and prompts us to action grows as we journey in this life, bringing us the assurance that we can change the world, or at least our little corner of it, with Christ's love. The freedom to express our faith in the God who loved us so much that he chose to die for us sends us forth to new life. But God is so good, for even after we have digested all of this, he presents us with the final course: eternal life.

Eternal life awaits those who believe in Christ as their Lord and Savior. As we turn from our sins and place them on the cross, as we are crucified with Christ, dying to our own desires and plans and being raised to new life in Christ with his desires and will for our lives, we look forward in anticipation to living eternally with him in heaven. "Today, you will be with me in paradise," Jesus told the thief who was crucified next to him. Christ told his followers that he was going to prepare a place for them in heaven, but he would return to take them home. We have that promise in this final part of the menu. Jesus will return for us. We will feast with him once again in heaven. But until that time, we can feast from his Easter menu and be filled with his presence every day of our lives for our God is a loving God.

This day is very special and has been blessed for it announces to the world the message of a Risen Lord. Eat hearty today from Christ's Easter menu. Be filled with his love and peace. Eat with him and eat of him through the Word and sacrament. Be filled with his forgiveness and power. Eat daily with him with grateful hearts honoring our Risen Lord. Be filled with thanksgiving to a God who rolled back the stones of our hearts and set us free to live in Christ. Eat and be filled never to hunger again. Eat and behold your Risen Lord. In his glorious and mighty name, Amen.

www.ingramcontent.com/pod-product-compliance
Lightning Source LLC
Chambersburg PA
CBHW060857050426
42453CB00008B/1006